VOCAL SELECTIONS

PETER PAN
MUSIC AND LYRICS BY
LEONARD BERNSTEIN
based on the book and play "Peter Pan" by J.M. Barrie

ISBN 978-1-4584-0026-0

The Name and Likeness of "Leonard Bernstein" is a registered trademark of Amberson Holdings LLC.
Used by Permission

LEONARD
BERNSTEIN
Music Publishing
Company LLC

BOOSEY & HAWKES

AN IMAGEM COMPANY

DISTRIBUTED BY

HAL•LEONARD®
CORPORATION
7777 W. BLUEMOUND RD. P.O. BOX 13819 MILWAUKEE, WI 53213

www.leonardbernstein.com
www.boosey.com
www.halleonard.com

LEONARD BERNSTEIN
AUGUST 25, 1918 - OCTOBER 14, 1990

Leonard Bernstein was born in Lawrence, Massachusetts. He took piano lessons as a boy and attended the Garrison and Boston Latin Schools. At Harvard University he studied with Walter Piston, Edward Burlingame-Hill, and A. Tillman Merritt, among others. Before graduating in 1939 he made an unofficial conducting debut with his own incidental music to the Aristophanes play *The Birds*, and directed and performed in Marc Blitzstein's *The Cradle Will Rock*. Subsequently, at the Curtis Institute of Music in Philadelphia, Bernstein studied piano with Isabella Vengerova, conducting with Fritz Reiner, and orchestration with Randall Thompson.

In 1940 Bernstein studied at the Boston Symphony Orchestra's newly created summer institute, Tanglewood, with the orchestra's conductor, Serge Koussevitzky. Bernstein later became Koussevitzky's conducting assistant. He made a sensational conducting debut with the New York Philharmonic in 1943. Bernstein became Music Director of the orchestra in 1958. From then until 1969 he led more concerts with the orchestra than any previous conductor. He subsequently held the lifetime title of Laureate Conductor, making frequent guest appearances with the orchestra. More than half of Bernstein's 400-plus recordings were made with the New York Philharmonic.

Bernstein traveled the world as a conductor. Immediately after World War II, in 1946, he conducted in London and at the International Music Festival in Prague. In 1947 he conducted in Tel Aviv, beginning a relationship with Israel that lasted until his death. In 1953 Bernstein was the first American to conduct opera at the Teatro alla Scala in Milan, in Cherubini's *Medea* with Maria Callas.

Beyond many distinguished achievements as a composer of concert works, Bernstein also wrote a one-act opera, *Trouble in Tahiti* (1952), and its sequel, the opera *A Quiet Place* (1983). He collaborated with choreographer Jerome Robbins on three major ballets: *Fancy Free* (1944), and *Facsimile* (1946) for American Ballet Theater, and *Dybbuk* (1974) for the New York City Ballet. Bernstein composed the score for the award-winning film *On the Waterfront* (1954) and incidental music for the Broadway play *The Lark* (1955).

Bernstein contributed substantially to the Broadway musical stage. He collaborated with Betty Comden and Adolph Green on *On the Town* (1944) and *Wonderful Town* (1953). For *Peter Pan* (1950) he penned his own lyrics to songs and also composed incidental music. In collaboration with Richard Wilbur, Lillian Hellman and others he wrote *Candide* (1956). Other versions of *Candide* were written in association with Hugh Wheeler, Stephen Sondheim and other lyricists. In 1957 he collaborated with Jerome Robbins, Stephen Sondheim and Arthur Laurents on the landmark musical *West Side Story*, which was made into an Academy Award-winning film. Bernstein also wrote the Broadway musical *1600 Pennsylvania Avenue* (1976) with lyricist Alan Jay Lerner.

In 1985 the National Academy of Recording Arts and Sciences honored Bernstein with the Lifetime Achievement Grammy Award. He won eleven Emmy Awards in his career. His televised concert and lecture series were launched with the "Omnibus" program in 1954, followed by the extraordinary "Young People's Concerts with the New York Philharmonic," which began in 1958 and extended over fourteen seasons. Among his many appearances on the PBS series "Great Performances" was the acclaimed eleven-part "Bernstein's Beethoven." In 1989 Bernstein and others commemorated the 1939 invasion of Poland in a worldwide telecast from Warsaw.

Bernstein's writings were published in *The Joy of Music* (1959), *Leonard Bernstein's Young People's Concerts* (1961), *The Infinite Variety of Music* (1966), and *Findings* (1982). Each has been widely translated. He gave six lectures at Harvard University in 1972-1973 as the Charles Eliot Norton Professor of Poetry. These lectures were subsequently published and televised as *The Unanswered Question*.

Bernstein received many honors. He was elected in 1981 to the American Academy of Arts and Letters, which gave him its Gold Medal. The National Fellowship Award in 1985 applauded his life-long support of humanitarian causes. He received the MacDowell Colony's Gold Medal; medals from the Beethoven Society and the Mahler Gesellschaft; the Handel Medallion, New York City's highest honor for the arts; a Tony award (1969) for Distinguished Achievement in the Theater; and dozens of honorary degrees and awards from colleges and universities. Bernstein was presented ceremonial keys to the cities of Oslo, Vienna, Bersheeva, and the village of Bernstein, Austria, among others. National honors came from Italy, Israel, Mexico, Denmark, Germany (the Great Merit Cross), and France (Chevalier, Officer and Commandeur of the Legion d'Honneur). Bernstein received the Kennedy Center Honors in 1980.

In 1990 Bernstein received the Praemium Imperiale, an international prize created in 1988 by the Japan Arts Association and awarded for lifetime achievement in the arts. He used the $100,000 prize to establish initiatives in the arts and education, principally the Leonard Bernstein Center for Artful Learning.

Bernstein was the father of three children — Jamie, Alexander and Nina — and enjoyed the arrival of his first two grandchildren, Francisca and Evan.

PETER PAN
TABLE OF CONTENTS

NOTES ON THE SHOW AND SONGS

PETER PAN

Play with music. Play by J.M. Barrie.
Incidental music and lyrics by Leonard Bernstein.
Broadway opening: April 24, 1950.

Who Am I?

Pirate Song

My House

Never-Land

Peter, Peter

Captain Hook's Soliloquy

Plank Round

Dream with Me

The character Peter Pan first appeared in a section of the 1902 novel *The Little White Bird* by Scottish writer J.M. Barrie (1860-1937). Barrie adapted the story for the stage in *Peter Pan*, or *The Boy Who Wouldn't Grow Up*, which was a big hit in London in 1904. Barrie again adapted the story and expanded it for the 1911 novel *Peter and Wendy*, later titled simply *Peter Pan*. The play became a popular classic in the UK and the US, with six Broadway productions between 1905 and 1928. A 1950 production, with movie star Jean Arthur as Peter, was its first in New York in 22 years. The production is decidedly a play with music, with songs and choruses, and not a full blown musical. It was originally intended as a musical, but the plan was made more modest due to the vocal limitations of Jean Arthur. *Peter Pan* has been the basis of many treatments, including a 1954 Mary Martin Broadway musical, completely different from the Bernstein version.

Lying in bed Wendy Darling wonders to herself **"Who Am I?"** as her two younger brothers are asleep. Peter Pan and his fairy Tinkerbell enter through the open window. Striking up a conversation with Wendy, the oldest, Peter shows her and her younger brothers, Michael and John, how they can fly by thinking lovely, wonderful thoughts. Peter then leads the three children over the city of London, past the "second star to the right and straight on till morning" to the magical land of Neverland. Peter and all the other Lost Boys who don't want to grow up live a wonderful life of jungle adventures in a tree house.

Enter the Pirates, led by the malicious Captain Hook **("Pirate Song")**. Hook lost his right arm to a crocodile when Peter Pan threw him into the reptile's jaws. The villain's greatest wish is to kill Peter as revenge. The same crocodile which ate Captain Hook's arm is on the prowl, always looking for Hook. His presence is made aware by the ticking sound of a clock, which he also once ate.

Wendy arrives in Neverland. She longs for a real home there, and in **"My House"** asks Peter to build it for her. The Lost Boys cannot remember their mothers, so they want Wendy to stay on as theirs. They ask her to be their mother and she accepts. Mermaids bask on a rock in the lagoon as they praise the wonders of **"Never-Land."** The Lost Boys go to sleep and Wendy and Peter are left alone. She shows her growing affection for him in **"Peter, Peter."** Many adventures ensue as the children try to avoid the menacing Captain Hook. Wendy and The Lost Boys are eventually captured and brought on board the pirate ship. Thinking he has poisoned Peter, Hook reflects on his life in **"Captain Hook's Soliloquy."** Hook and the Pirates revel in the glories of the plank **("Plank Round")**. After a battle with Peter, Captain Hook is eaten by the crocodile. All the orphaned Lost Boys come to live with the Darling family, but Peter decides to stay in Neverland, remaining a boy forever.

"Dream with Me" was written for the production but cut, and was not publicly performed until 1975, when it was included in the 1975 Off-Broadway revue *By Bernstein* (withdrawn by the composer)."

BERNSTEIN'S PETER PAN

The history of Leonard Bernstein's songs and incidental music for J.M. Barrie's play *Peter Pan* is a complicated one. His involvement in the 1950 Broadway production, starring Boris Karloff and Jean Arthur, was relatively minimal in comparison to his other Broadway works. Invited to provide only a few dances and incidental cues, he found himself "losing his head," and surprised the producers by writing seven songs as well, including original lyrics. Bernstein was in Europe during the rehearsal period for the show, unable to participate in the creative process as he usually would for a new theatre work. It was Trude Rittman, credited as Musical Coordinator, who took his material and worked it into the production according to its needs, extracting reprises and underscores from Bernstein's larger numbers and adapting Tink's musical speech fragments to fit the play dialogue. This *Peter Pan* is not a musical – Bernstein did not structure a musical/dramatic totality as he did for his other stage works, and was not a direct collaborator in the production. Nevertheless, the score demonstrates a clear use of motivic development, and a consistency of gesture, innocence, and wit that together form a cohesive whole.

Many curious changes were made to the score after it left Bernstein's hands. The lovely "Dream with Me" was jettisoned as Wendy's final song, in favor of an inexplicable reprise of "Who Am I." An additional scene was created for the death of Hook (not included in the vocal score, or for that matter in the play itself) which sutured "Plank Round" and "Never-Land" together with new lyrics of dubious authorship (they were certainly not written by Bernstein or Barrie), to provide a pat moral to this morally ambiguous story. For the original cast recording, Bernstein's instrumental numbers, for reasons unknown, were replaced with new cues by Alec Wilder (which has led to the misconception that Bernstein's incidental music was not used for the Broadway production), and the songs themselves were altered to accommodate spoken narration and new introductions. Many of these recording-specific alterations to the songs were in turn re-incorporated into the orchestral materials for the show. For the national tour, with Lawrence Tibbett as Hook, Bernstein contributed a new song, "Captain Hook's Soliloquy," but the tour was cancelled mid-run, and the song went unheard for decades.

Bernstein's music for *Peter Pan* lay fallow for over half a century, largely forgotten save for a very few sporadic, small-scale productions, and overshadowed by the 1954 full-blown musical treatment (with lyrics by Carolyn Leigh, Betty Comden and Adolph Green, music by Mark Charlap and Jule Styne, and direction and choreography by Jerome Robbins, Bernstein's long-time friends and collaborators). But in 2001, the conductor Alexander Frey came to the Leonard Bernstein Office with the proposal to record the score in its entirety, including "Dream with Me" and "Captain Hook's Soliloquy," for which new orchestrations were created by Sid Ramin and myself. The recording has been a great success, leading to the first significant theatrical productions in over a generation.

Garth Edwin Sunderland

Who Am I?

Music and Lyrics by
LEONARD BERNSTEIN

Refrain

Who am I? Was it all planned in ad- vance or was

I just born by chance in Ju - ly? Oh, who on Earth am I? Did I

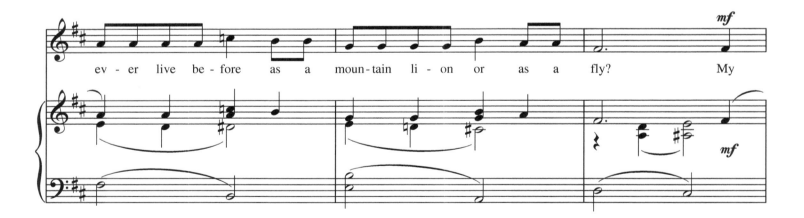

ev - er live be- fore as a moun- tain li - on or as a fly? My

friends on - ly think of fun, they're all such in - cur - a - ble tots! Can

I be the on-ly one who thinks these mys-ter-i-ous thoughts? Some

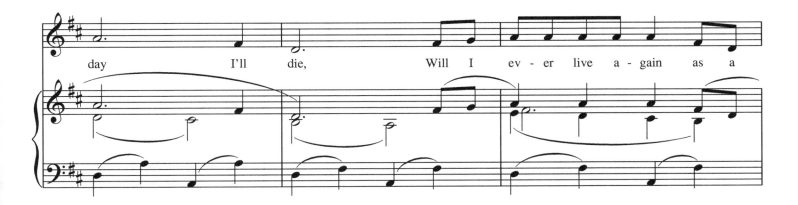

day I'll die, Will I ev-er live a-gain as a

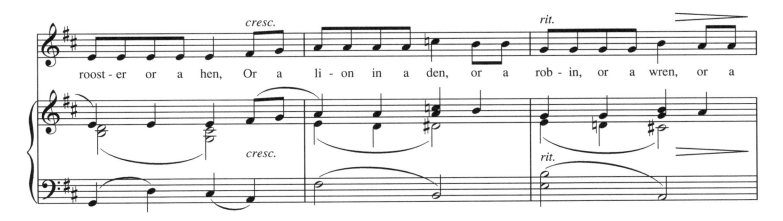

roost-er or a hen, Or a li-on in a den, or a rob-in, or a wren, or a

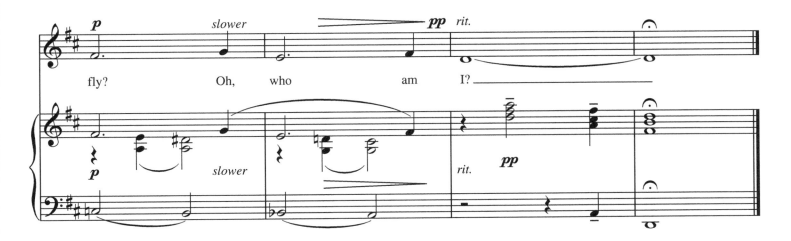

fly? Oh, who am I?

Pirate Song

Ensemble for Baritone Solo, Tenors, and Basses

Music and Lyrics by
LEONARD BERNSTEIN

It is true that the bass - es have e - vil - er fac - es, but

ten - ors are!

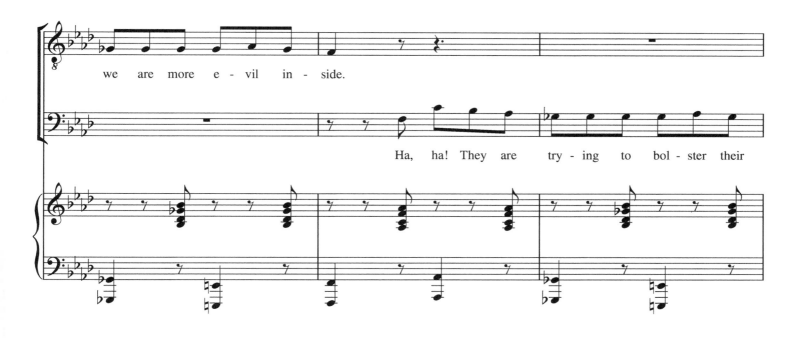

we are more e - vil in - side.

Ha, ha! They are try - ing to bol - ster their

Not true! Our sweet voic - es are just a dis - guise!

pride!

Ha, ha! Their good -

Not true! Our sweet voic - es are just a dis -
heart - ed - ness shines in their eyes! Ha, ha! Their good

guise! Not true! Our sweet voic - es are just a dis - guise! Not true! Our sweet
heart - ed - ness shines in their eyes! Ha, ha! Their good heart - ed - ness shines in their

vamp

voic - es are just a dis - guise! Not true! Our sweet voic - es are just a dis -
eyes! Ha, ha! Their good heart - ed - ness shines in their eyes! Ha, ha! Their good

top note only

vamp

stuff! When I am a - round there's no ques - tion of who has the

mean - est, the low - est, the loath - some - est, cru - el - est look. It's Hook!

Aye, aye! Aye,

Aye, aye! Aye,

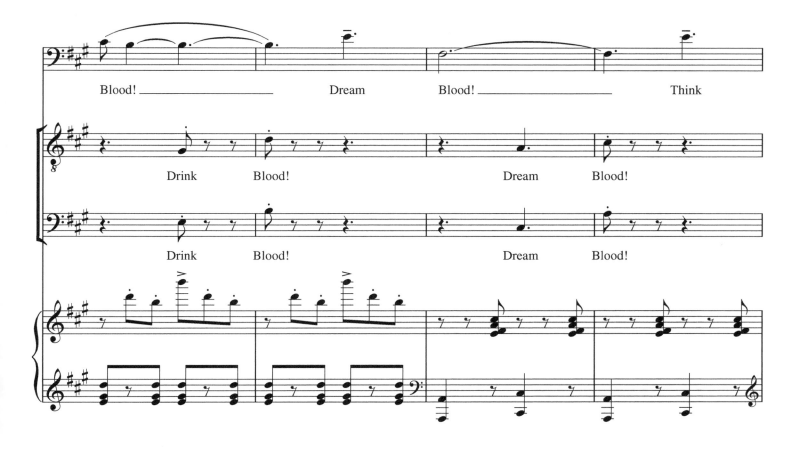

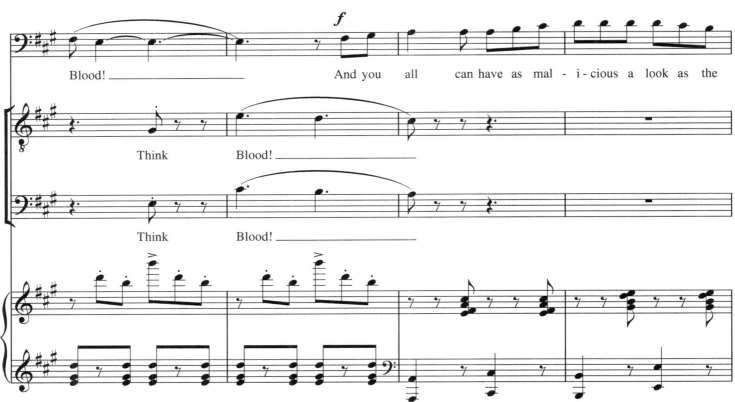

Blood! _____ And you all can have as mal - i - cious a look as the

Think Blood! _____

Think Blood! _____

mean - est of all, Cap - tain Hook! Eat

Aye, aye! The mean - est is Cap - tain Hook!

Aye, aye! The mean - est is Cap - tain Hook!

top note only

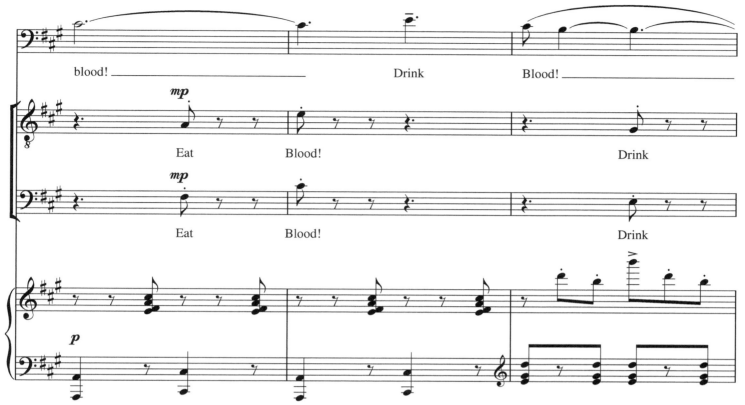

blood! _____ Drink Blood! _____

Eat Blood! Drink

Eat Blood! Drink

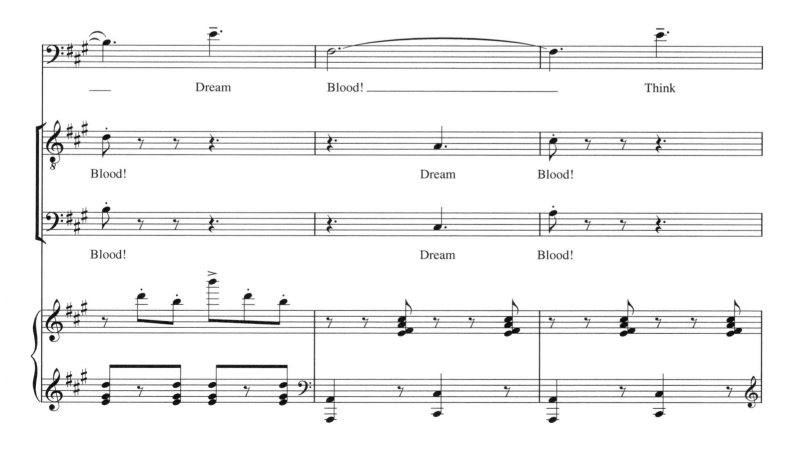

__ Dream Blood! _____ Think

Blood! Dream Blood!

Blood! Dream Blood!

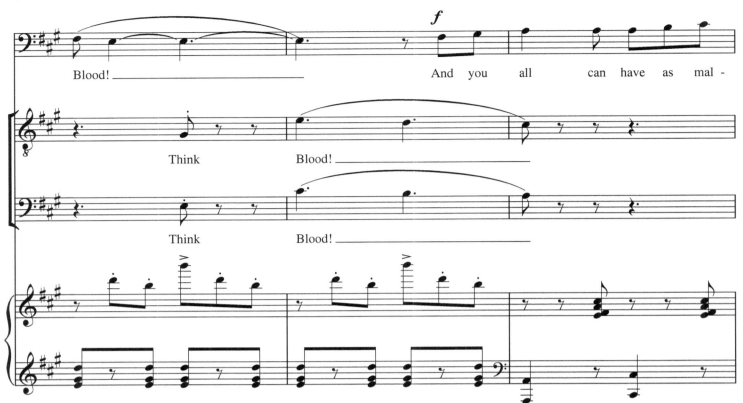

Blood! _____ And you all can have as mal-

Think   Blood! _____

Think   Blood! _____

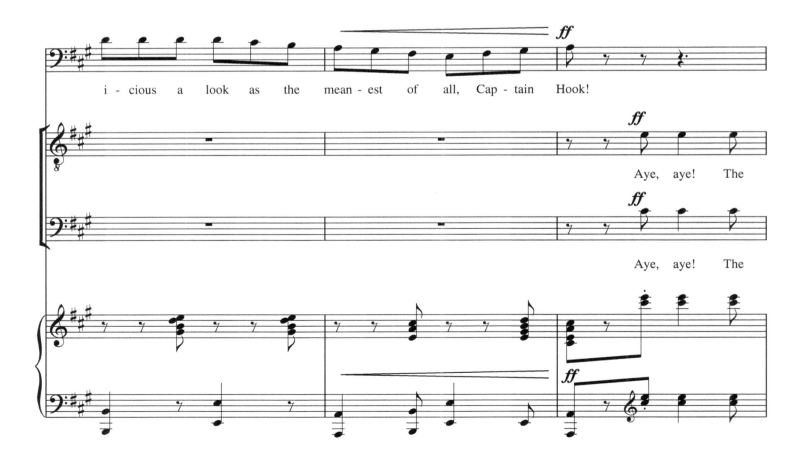

i - cious a look as the mean-est of all, Cap-tain Hook!

Aye, aye! The

Aye, aye! The

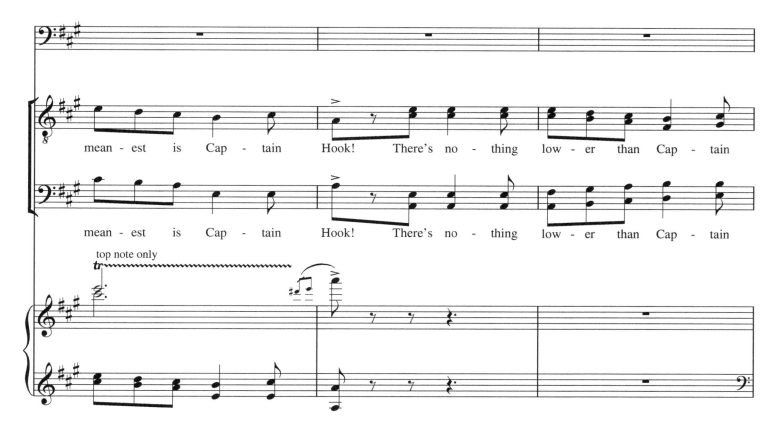

mean - est is Cap - tain Hook! There's no - thing low - er than Cap - tain

mean - est is Cap - tain Hook! There's no - thing low - er than Cap - tain

top note only

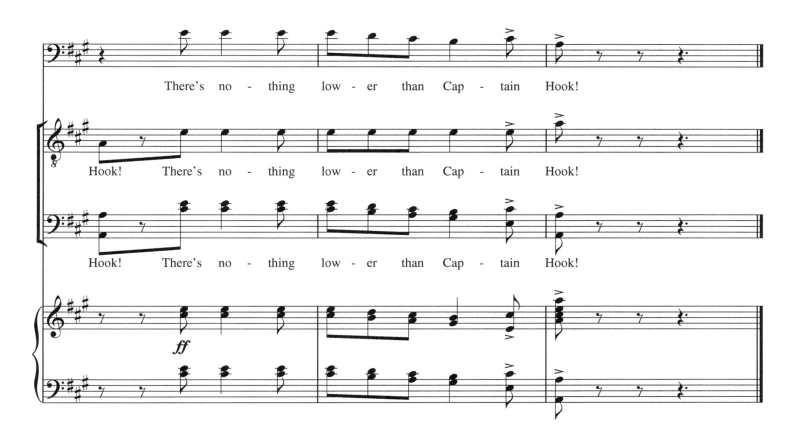

There's no - thing low - er than Cap - tain Hook!

Hook! There's no - thing low - er than Cap - tain Hook!

Hook! There's no - thing low - er than Cap - tain Hook!

My House

Music and Lyrics by
LEONARD BERNSTEIN

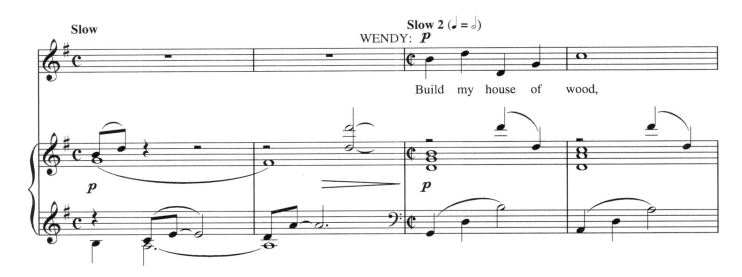

Strong a - gainst the storm. Shel - ter when the days grow

poco più mosso
poco a poco cresc.

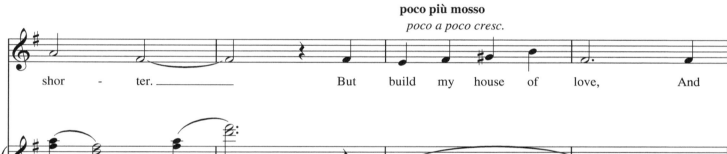

shor - ter. _____ But build my house of love, And

paint my house with trust - ing, And warm it with the warmth of your

cresc. *f*

heart. _____ Make the floor of faith,

Make the walls of truth, Put a roof of peace a -

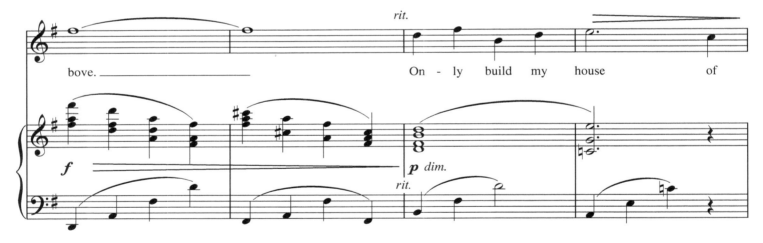

bove. _____ On - ly build my house of

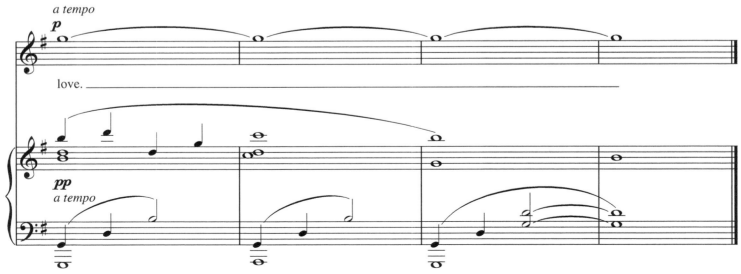

love. _____

Never-Land
Duet for 2 Sopranos

Music and Lyrics by
LEONARD BERNSTEIN

Moderato (♩ = 88)

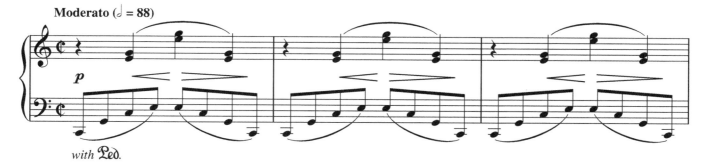

with Ped.

MERMAIDS:

This has been a love-ly day of sun and sand ___

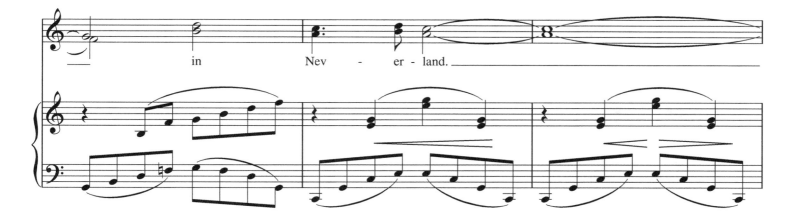

___ in Nev-er-land. ___

Eight-een hours of

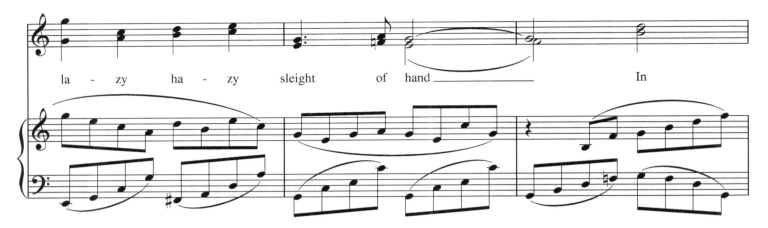

la - zy ha - zy sleight of hand _____ In

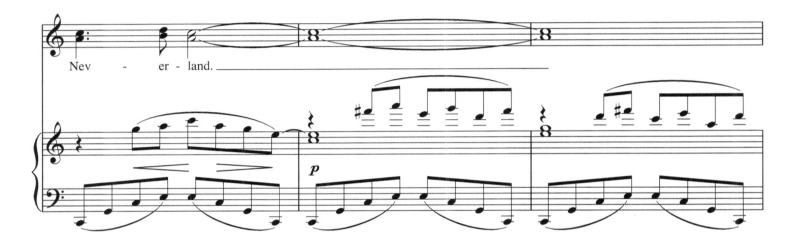

Nev - er - land. _____

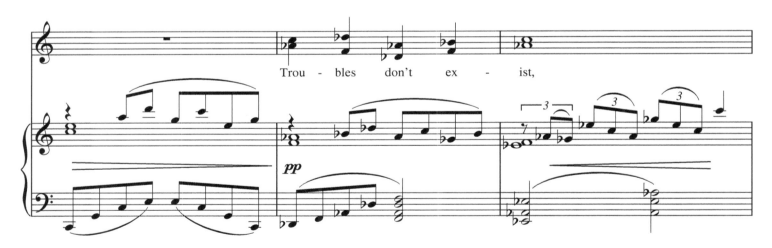

Trou - bles don't ex - ist,

No one is a pes - si - mist, Ev - 'ry one's ex -

act - ly what he wants to be._____

_____ Here it nev - er

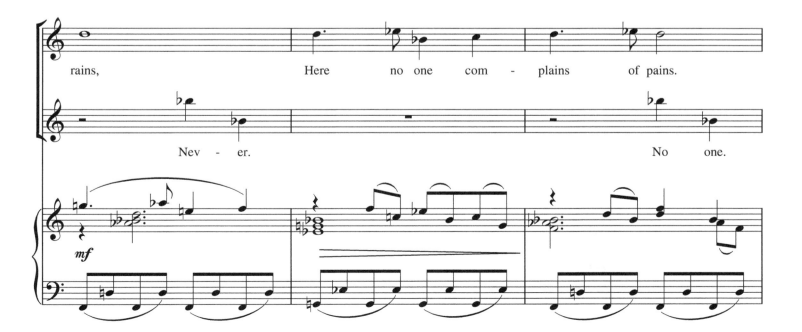

rains, Here no one com - plains of pains.

Nev - er. No one.

20

Child - ish hearts re - joic - ing in their fan - ta - sy._____

Child - ish hearts re - joic - ing in their fan - ta - sy._____

Love - ly la - zy day of sea and sun and sand_____

For ev - er and _____

ev - er and ev - er in Nev - er - land. _____

p

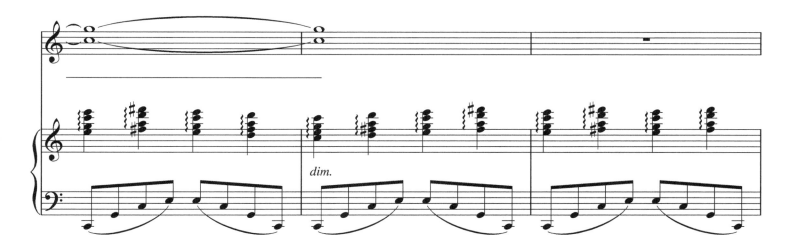

dim.

(dim.)

vuota

as mermaids
jump into lagoon

ff

Peter, Peter

Music and Lyrics by
LEONARD BERNSTEIN

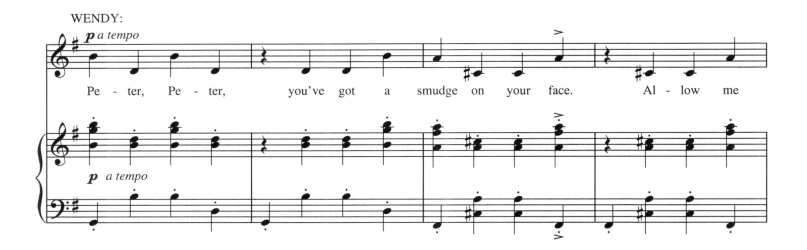

just an old ex - cuse to feel your touch, Well I want to feel your

touch! Pe - ter, Pe - ter, your hair is all out of place;

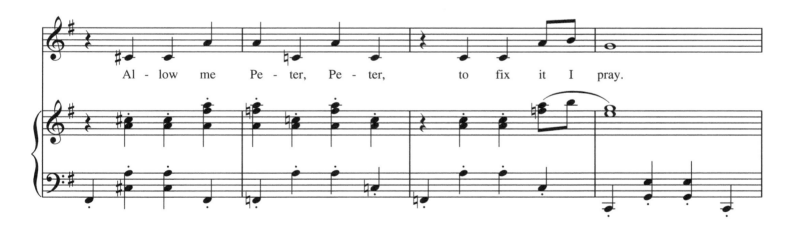

Al - low me Pe - ter, Pe - ter, to fix it I pray.

I have to feel you to make sure you're real - ly real,

Just a lit-tle ti-ny feel. The touch of you, ____

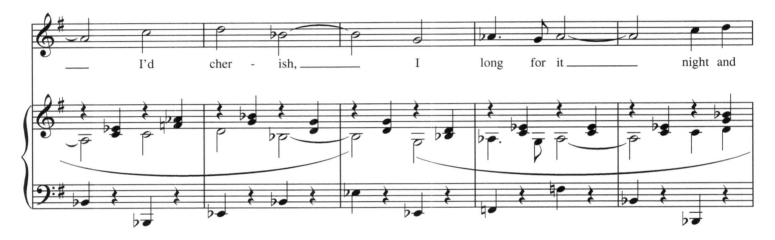

____ I'd cher - ish, _____ I long for it _____ night and

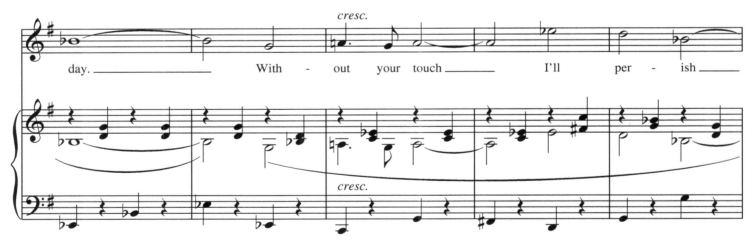

day. _____ With - out your touch _____ I'll per - ish _____

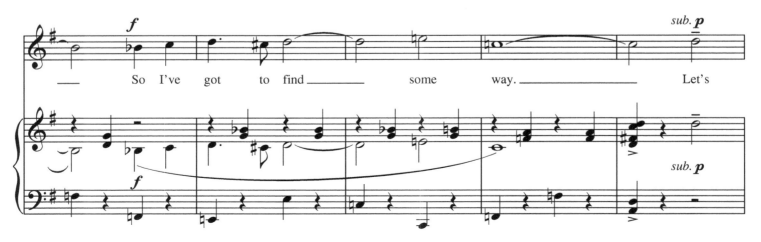

____ So I've got to find _____ some way. _____ Let's

see, It's real - ly true. Be - lieve me

Pe - ter, Pe - ter, you've got a mos - qui - to on you, Al - right it's

just a poor ex - cuse to feel your touch. Yes I want to feel your

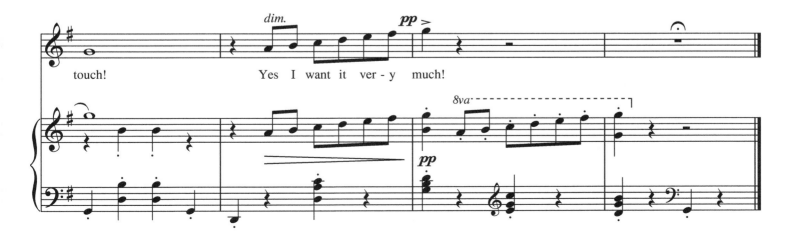

touch! Yes I want it ver - y much!

for Lawrence Tibbett
with admiration

Captain Hook's Soliloquy
(Recitative and Aria)

Lyrics by
JAMES M. BARRIE

Music by
LEONARD BERNSTEIN

Presto furioso (♩. = 132)

(Captain Hook gazes quietly into the moonlight, undisturbed by orchestral goings-on.)

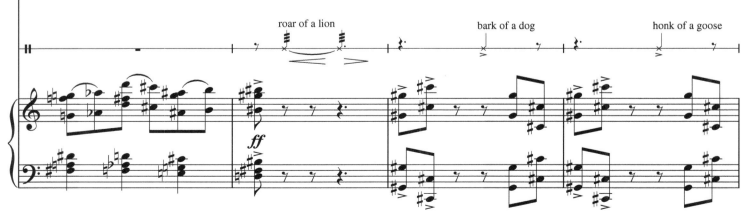

meow of a cat

grunt of a pig or frog

monkey cry

Adagio (recit. a piacere)

p mezza voce

CAPTAIN HOOK:

Presto (come prima)

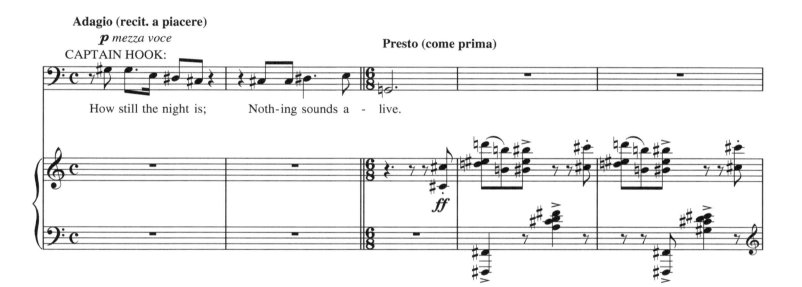

How still the night is; Noth-ing sounds a - live.

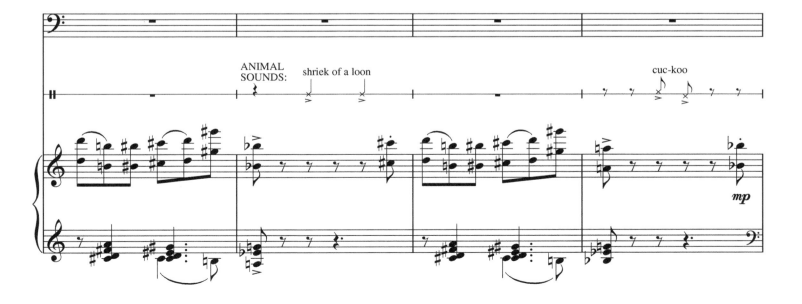

ANIMAL SOUNDS: shriek of a loon

cuc-koo

roar of a lion

cresc. molto

ff

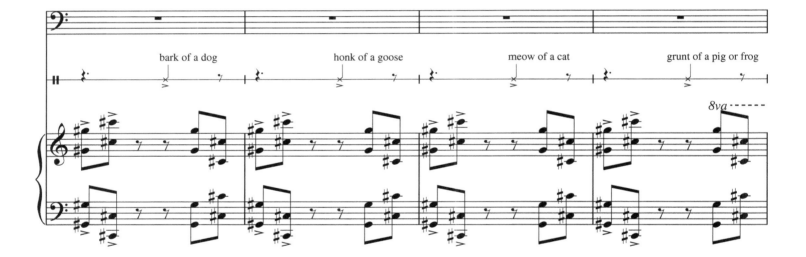

bark of a dog honk of a goose meow of a cat grunt of a pig or frog

8va

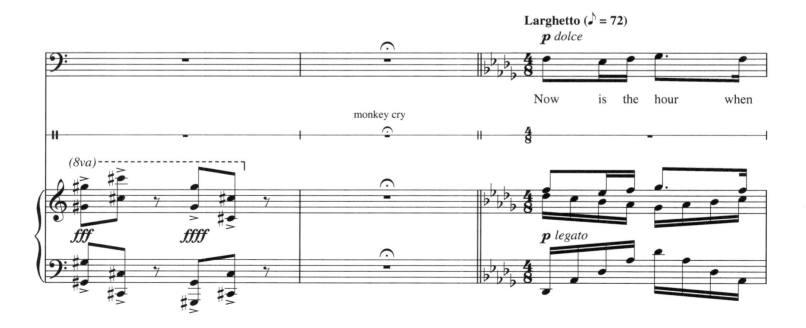

Larghetto (♪ = 72)
p dolce

Now is the hour when

monkey cry

fff *ffff*

p legato

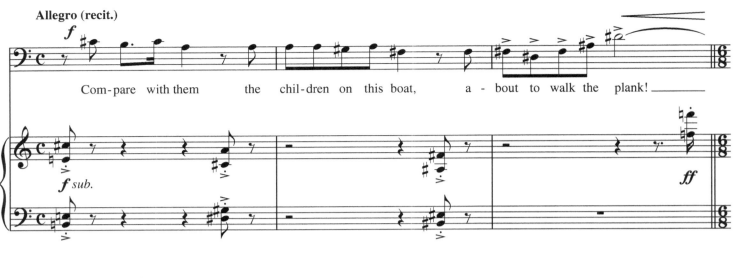

Allegro (recit.)

Com- pare with them the chil- dren on this boat, a - bout to walk the plank! _____

Presto (come prima)

agitato

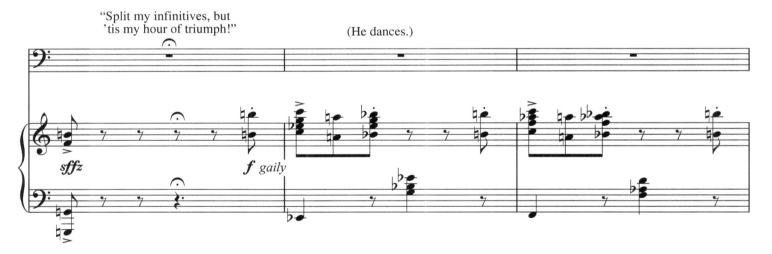

"Split my infinitives, but
'tis my hour of triumph!"

(He dances.)

f gaily

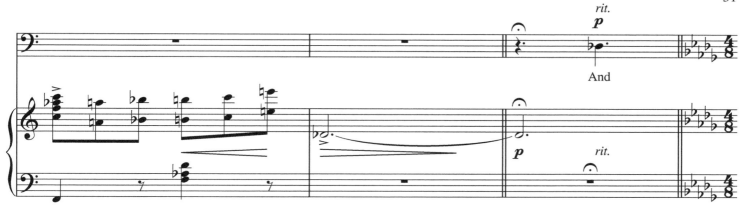

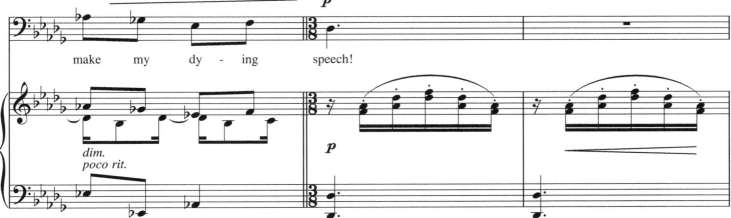

All mor - tals en - vy me, All mor - tals

en - vy me, yet bet - ter, bet - ter per - haps for Hook, to have had

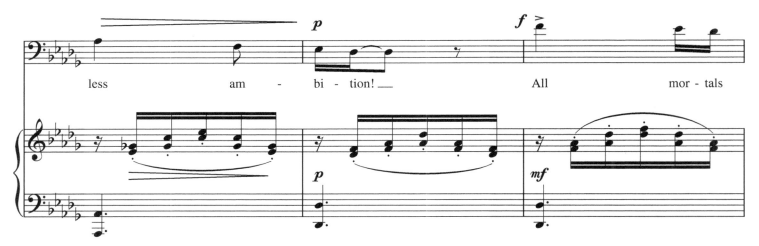

less am - bi - tion! __ All mor - tals

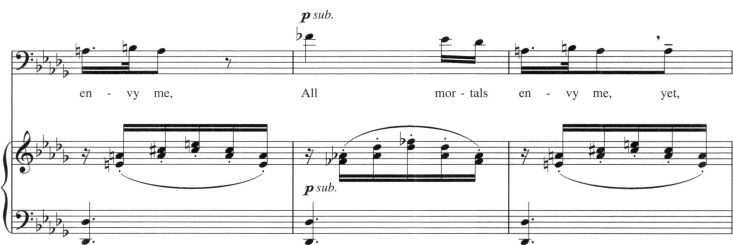

en - vy me, All mor - tals en - vy me, yet,

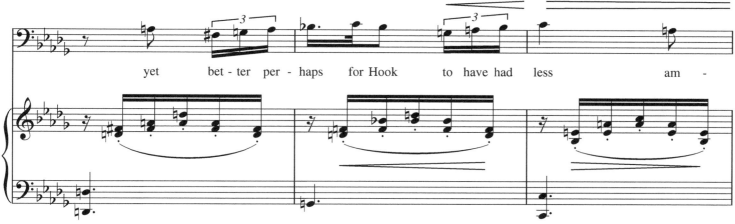

yet bet - ter per - haps for Hook to have had less am -

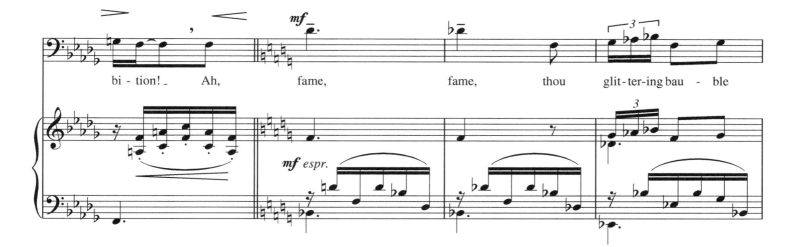

bi - tion! _ Ah, fame, fame, thou glit - ter - ing bau - ble

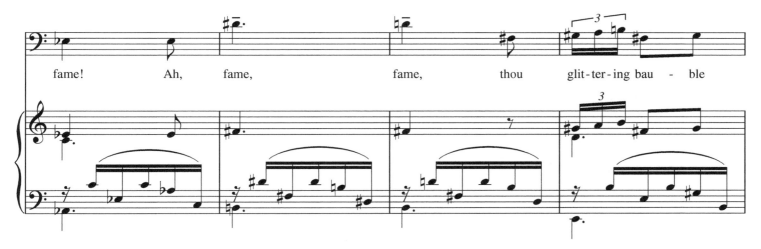

fame! Ah, fame, fame, thou glit - ter - ing bau - ble

fame! Thou glit - ter - ing bau - ble fame! Thou glit - ter - ing bau - ble

fame, what if the ver - y ma -

Cadenza *(collapsing)* *a tempo*

Fame, fame, thou glit - ter - ing bau - ble!

a tempo
cantabile

p quasi parlando (mezza voce)

No lit - tle chil - dren love me. I am told they play at Pe - ter

Pan, and that the strong - est al - ways choos - es to be

Plank Round

Ensemble for Baritone Solo, Tenors, and Basses

Music and Lyrics by
LEONARD BERNSTEIN

*pronounced "bo-sun"

1, 2

3

2. We
3. There

dim.

ff

Dream with Me

Music and Lyrics by
LEONARD BERNSTEIN

A separate publication of "Dream with Me" is available for voice, cello and piano.

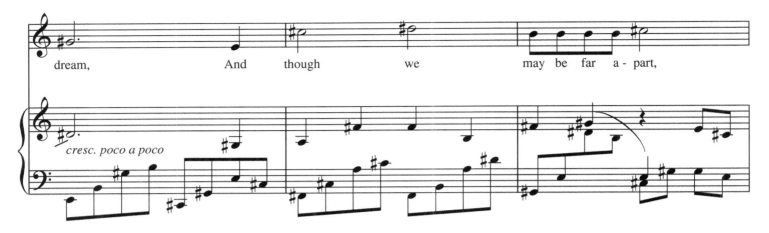

dream, And though we may be far a-part,

Keep me in your heart and dream with me. The kiss we nev - er dared

we'll dare in dream - ing. The love we

nev - er shared can still have mean - ing.

If you on-ly dream a mag-ic dream with me to - night, To -

night and ev - 'ry night, Wher - ev - er you may chance to

be, Close your love-ly eyes and dream with me.

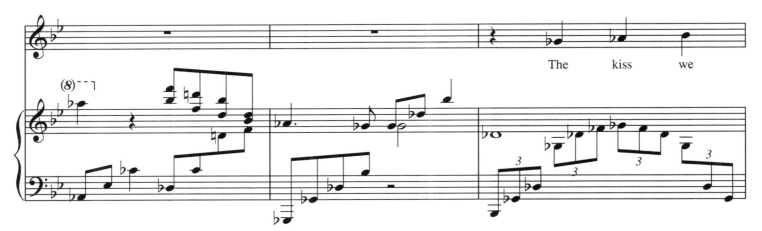

The kiss we

nev - er dared _____ we'll dare in dream - ing.

The love we nev - er shared _____ can still have

mean - ing. If you on - ly dream a mag - ic